The Celestial Helix

And Other One-Act Plays

by Anita Higman

Lillenas PUBLISHING COMPANY

KANSAS CITY, MO 64141

Lillenas Publishing Company
P.O. Box 419527
Kansas City, MO 64141
phone: 816-931-1900 • fax: 816-753-4071
E-mail: drama@lillenas.com

Printed in United States.

Cover art by Paul Franitza

DEDICATION

To Rev. Richard Ryan
and to Sue Woertz

Thank you for being part of the dream . . .
For breathing a special life into my characters,
Pokeweed Jones and Gloria Gasp

Contents

Foreword

I have spent my academic life where I was professor of drama at Southern Nazarene University when Anita was my student, and my professional life as a playwright of 69 three-act plays and 33 full-scale musicals learning this vital truth:

Drama invites
the human heart
to the greatest degree
of vulnerability
of all
media.

This is an extreme statement. **I believe it.**

It is true, of course, that lives are transformed, enriched, motivated by each medium. It is true that each medium has its place. **But drama has a unique power.**

Only experience through drama can allow a human heart to touch, to feel, to know the courage beyond fear, to grasp life-splinters and to make a new wholeness impossible beyond faith, and to think in spans 10,000 years of humanity striving to find God in personal terms. In the vulnerability of drama, I can lay aside all my carefully plastered masks and step into the heartbeat of another and, there, have the freedom to scoop up the debris of my life and of my times and carefully observe the giant human spirit to be more, more, more than can ever be imagined in the finite.

In drama God enables me to step from my familiar terrain and step into the unknown, into the unexplored, into the unseen.

I believe you will find that these plays written by Anita Higman can be an invitation to your audiences to explore the human experience and to be enriched through this God-given gift called drama.

Ruth Vaughn
Oklahoma City, Oklahoma

Introduction

I have always loved pretending.

When I was a kid growing up in the country, imagining fantastic events reigned supreme on my list of favorite things. I could do anything in my imagination. My stacked mud pies were transformed into a glorious wedding cake, fishing in our creek took on a dangerous feel of wild adventure, and the kitchen window suddenly became a television camera, so that our entire farm world could experience my impromptu commercials.

As an adult my mind still loves to wonder. I like to create unusual yet relatable happenings with words. I like to think of very different people being thrown together and then watch how they collide and cope and then care for each other. I like to imagine characters saying thought-provoking and unexpected things, yet the real-people-stuff that we can't believe how much it sounds like our Uncle Joe or that friend down the street.

Drama is us. It is all of us. It is the stew of life we are all boiling and sinking and floating in. But there is reason in all that swirling mixture.

Drama can make us see each other more clearly. Drama is capable of making us look up and ponder. At its best, it can make us think of new ways to understand and love, and perhaps briefly touch the very finger of God. Drama can be invigorating . . . inspiring . . . life-changing. I love it just as I loved pretending all those many years ago. Drama is a magnificent gift from God, and I am grateful to help celebrate its wonder and beauty with each of you.

(I also thank God for childhood, imaginations, and yes, even mud pies!)

Anita Higman
Houston

The Celestial Helix

A Drama in One Act

Insider Information

The *Helix* sprang up from many different sources. Sometimes drama is not so much extracted from one's own personal realities as it is the compilation of truths and observations of life in general.

Even though I have not experienced the trauma that the character Constance suffers from, we have all seen the pain of many people with similar life struggles. Not always is there a happy ending in real life, but it seemed right and good to give this piece a hope-filled conclusion.

Cast: Three females; one male

CONSTANCE: Constance Rutherford Thorpe is a wealthy 45-year-old alcoholic. Constance has reached a point of desperation in her life. She wants to make a positive difference in the world but is afraid of changing her lifestyle and that of her family. This dilemma gradually brought on her drinking, which now compounds her problem. Constance speaks without an accent.

LIZZY: Lizzy is a 30-year-old female actor who is currently working at the Thorpe Playhouse. She is dressed as a bag lady, researching a role as a homeless woman for an upcoming production at the Thorpe Playhouse. Lizzy has no natural accent but improvises with a Bronx and Texas accent while researching her role as a bag lady.

RITA: Rita is a female actor in her late 20s who is also researching a role as a homeless woman for the upcoming production at the Thorpe Playhouse. Rita and Lizzy have been longtime friends. Rita speaks without an accent.

JOHN: John Thorpe is Constance's husband. He is a successful middle-aged psychiatrist. He loves Constance but has become so involved with his work that he hasn't taken time to consider her needs or desires. Rationalization has caused John to brush aside any fears he might have of Constance becoming an alcoholic or suicidal. John speaks without an accent.

Scene: We are at a bus stop in a large Southern city.

Time: It is evening in the present.

Props:

    General: Bus stop sign
        Bus stop bench
        Trash receptacle

    Constance: Small evening bag with diamond-looking stones on front
        Wristwatch
        Small paper bag of groceries
            a. 1 full bottle of "liquor"
            b. 1 full bottle of rubbing alcohol
            c. 3 jars of olives

    Lizzy: Large mesh or old canvas bag
        Miscellaneous belongings for bag
        Play script

    Rita: Old canvas bag of belongings
        Old hat

No sound effects or special lighting required.

Approximate playing time: 35 minutes.

(We are at a bus stop in a large Southern city. A bench is CS, a trash receptacle is LC, and bus stop sign is RC. It is evening in the present. LIZZY is standing near the bench at the bus stop. She is dressed like a bag lady with tattered clothes and a dirty face. She is holding an open play script. On the bench is a large mesh bag that appears to contain her few belongings.

    (At rise of the curtain, LIZZY is walking around the bus stop bench, reciting some of her lines from the play script she is holding.)

LIZZY *(four-line script recited with a Bronx accent):* Frankie, it's your empty pride that's keeping our stomachs empty. I'm going back to begging for food. And if that pains your delicate sensibilities . . . then go . . . and take your never-never land with you.

(LIZZY notices a woman approaching, so she quickly hides her script in her mesh bag. LIZZY sits down at one end of the bench. She assumes a slightly crouched posture, trying to appear old and tired. CONSTANCE enters SR. CONSTANCE is very well groomed and is wearing a sequined evening gown. She is carrying an evening bag and a small paper bag of groceries. CONSTANCE eyes LIZZY suspiciously and then approaches the bus stop bench cautiously. CONSTANCE reluctantly sits down on the bench at the opposite end from LIZZY. CONSTANCE continually checks her watch nervously.)

LIZZY *(speaking tiredly, using a moderate Texas accent; looks over at CONSTANCE curiously):* Tell me, do you always dress like that to ride the bus?

CONSTANCE (*hesitates in responding or even looking at* LIZZY): I'm not here to ride the bus.

LIZZY (*rises and moves away from* CONSTANCE): Oh. Excuse me, I don't like getting involved with "that."

CONSTANCE (*keeps looking at her watch and becoming more nervous about her conversation with* LIZZY): I beg your pardon?

LIZZY: Well, women in this part of town only dress like that for one reason, and it's not 'cause they're making time for the opera. They're just making time. The cops will be dragging you away in a few minutes. I don't want to be seen in any tête-à-tête with you.

CONSTANCE: I am not what you think I am. You are speaking with one of the wealthiest women in this city. I come from a long line of Rutherfords.

LIZZY: Well, you are talking to one of the poorest women in this city, and I came from a long line too . . . it's called a bread line. You should try it sometime. Their soup du jour is always so yummy you don't even notice the mouse dung floating in it.

CONSTANCE: I'm sorry.

LIZZY (*pronounces each letter of acronym, "L.S.A."*): Not as sorry as you're going to be when the police book you up on an L.S.A. . . .

CONSTANCE: What is that?

LIZZY: "Loitering in Suspicious Apparel."

CONSTANCE: I've never heard of such a thing. And I'm not loitering. I was driving from the grocery store when my car ran out of gas. I'm merely waiting on my husband. (*Checks her watch again and picks imaginary lint off her dress*) He should be here any moment to rescue me.

LIZZY: Rescue you from what? You're just sitting on a bench.

CONSTANCE: Yes, but I'm not accustomed to being alone in the bad part of town. I could fall prey to some carousing fugitive. They murder people, you know. (*Takes a deep breath at each pause*) I'll just take some slow, deep breaths . . . and before I know it . . . all of this will be nothing more than a humorous anecdote at my party tonight . . .

LIZZY (*sarcastically*): To think, I'll be part of a humorous anecdote at a party in one of the richest homes in America. Now my life is complete.

CONSTANCE: I'm sorry. I didn't really mean that comment about the anecdote *personally*.

LIZZY: Oh. I guess you just meant it impersonally. (*Pause*) So why did you go to the grocery store yourself? I'm surprised you don't have servants to do that.

CONSTANCE: I do. *(Looks at her watch nervously)* I really don't have time for this. I'm supposed to be home. I have guests arriving in less than an hour.

LIZZY *(sits back down on bench and says sarcastically):* Well, I'd help you out, but I gave my chauffeur the night off.

CONSTANCE: That is exactly why I'm in this mess. I gave my chauffeur the day off because of his father's funeral, and now here I am. My friends all say I'm much too altruistic for my own good.

LIZZY: Sounds like you're heading for an H.B.O. . . .

CONSTANCE: What is an H.B.O.?

LIZZY: "Humanitarian Burn Out."

CONSTANCE: You're making fun of me.

LIZZY *(sarcastically):* Well, I didn't mean it *personally.* *(Pause)* So what's this party you're having?

CONSTANCE: If you must know, it's for The Sweet Heart Ladies Charity Society and their husbands. I'm the social chairperson, and several times a year I have an appreciation celebration for them. We all work very hard.

LIZZY: Your days must be grueling. All those charity activities and still finding time to accessorize doggy's wardrobe. I just don't know how you people do it.

CONSTANCE: I will endure yet another false accusation to explain that our charity is out there helping people like yourself. Our pledge is to *purge* this city of hunger and declare war on homelessness.

LIZZY *(gradually breaks character more and more, because of her inner need to lash out at her mother, whom* CONSTANCE *reminds her of):* I know you better than you think I do.

CONSTANCE: You've heard of us then?

LIZZY: I went to your palatial headquarters one time and helped myself to some apples. I was suddenly *purged* from the building by two security guards. So, I guess you *have* declared war . . . and it seems I am one of the casualties.

CONSTANCE: I'm sorry you had that experience, but you must go through the proper procedures to receive assistance. We have some paperwork that's necessary to ensure that no one abuses the system.

LIZZY: Well, one of life's brutal facts is that when you're starving for something, be it love or food, you don't give a flying fig about proper procedures.

CONSTANCE: I've known hunger a few times, so I understand.

LIZZY: Yes, it's a ghastly wait between breakfast and brunch.

CONSTANCE: That's not fair.

LIZZY: Fair is for fairy tales.

CONSTANCE: Despite your unfortunate encounter with our charity group, I still believe we do many productive things.

LIZZY: Yes, you do. You produce stacks of paperwork for the hapless have-nots, so they can be neatly filed away into oblivion.

CONSTANCE: You know, all this complaining doesn't help anyone.

LIZZY: Least of all you, right? I guess charity and complaints aren't as satisfying as those good ol' capital gains. That's what your parties are all about. Since you can't squeeze much financial benefit or hero worship out of us, you resort to a few self-indulgent evenings of glory.

CONSTANCE: All I want to know is, whatever happened to a thankful heart?

LIZZY: I guess it got eaten by a hungry stomach.

CONSTANCE: You've mentioned hunger several times now. I am concerned, but I don't want to humiliate you by giving you money for food.

LIZZY (sarcastically): It's encouraging to meet so many people who are concerned about my feelings . . . makes me proud to be a starving American.

CONSTANCE: I don't understand you.

LIZZY: It's people like you that are misunderstanding us to death.

CONSTANCE (genuinely): What if I said I truly want to understand?

LIZZY: Oh. Now you're going to get syrupy? Right?

CONSTANCE: I see. It appears either way I'm doomed.

LIZZY: If you mean condemned to everlasting punishment, that's between you and God.

CONSTANCE: You think I'm no better than the devil, don't you?

LIZZY: I think your just deserts will be served to you . . . but it won't be cherries jubilee.

CONSTANCE: But you don't even know me.

LIZZY: When the soul doth fall, the eyes tell all . . . vanity, lack of compassion, self-indulgence. It's all right there in living color.

CONSTANCE (lightly skeptical): I suppose you can tell how much oat bran I eat too.

LIZZY: You don't eat oat bran.

CONSTANCE *(becoming concerned that* LIZZY *really can see into her soul):* No I don't. *(Pause)* What else can you see?

LIZZY: Oh, whether or not you have a G.T.F.W. . . .

CONSTANCE *(mildly skeptical):* And what is that?

LIZZY: A "Genetic Tendency for Facial Warts." *(Chuckles at her own joke)*

CONSTANCE: That's the last time you're getting me with one of those.

LIZZY: Seriously, you can tell where a person is on "life's helix" just by staring into their eyes. Do you know what a helix is?

CONSTANCE: Of course I do. It's a spiral like a corkscrew.

LIZZY *(patronizingly):* Very good. *(Waits for* CONSTANCE *to ask about "life's helix")*

CONSTANCE *(trying to hide her interest):* I'm surprised you're not going to explain "life's helix."

LIZZY *(rises, walks behind* CONSTANCE, *and leans in near her, sounding mysterious):* Consider this . . . if people weren't so consumed with their own lives, they'd discover that every living soul is alike in one very sobering way. We are all born into the middle of a helix . . . a winding, inescapable course of choices. Truth and God are at one end of the spiral . . . and we all know what's at the other end, don't we? It's not like a sweet dream or a paradoxical nightmare that vaporizes in the morning. It's real, with consequences every second we're alive . . . or dead. *(Sits back down and says lightly)* So *that,* my fine sequined friend, is what "life's helix" is.

CONSTANCE *(said to the side):* If only I hadn't asked. *(Directly to* LIZZY) By the way, isn't your analogy a bit simplistic and curiously serpentine?

LIZZY: It's only simple to the simpleminded, and "life's helix" may be serpentine to you but it's a celestial spiral to those with a clear conscience.

CONSTANCE: Are you absolutely certain you're a bag lady?

LIZZY *(holds up her mesh bag):* Well, I'm a lady, and I've got a bag. I guess that makes me a bag lady. What did you expect anyway? A toothless drunk who mumbles incoherently in double negatives and smells like sewer gas?

CONSTANCE: I don't know.

(There's an uncomfortable silence between them as they take turns staring at each other.)

CONSTANCE: You have a long wait for the bus. If you'd like, my husband and I could give you a life wherever you want to go.

LIZZY: Your Freudian slip just bought me a life.

CONSTANCE: A life? What do you mean? I said we'd give you a lift anywhere you . . . *(With confusion)* Perhaps I did say life.

LIZZY: I wouldn't want what you call "a life" anyway.

CONSTANCE: My offer still stands about the lift. It'll be a long wait for the bus, so I'd be more than—

LIZZY *(interrupting):* I'm not waiting on the bus.

CONSTANCE: Do you have someone to drive you where you need to go?

LIZZY: Why is it people must be constantly going somewhere or coming from somewhere or waiting on something to make them feel worthy to exist? *(Pause)* Oh, why not? If I must wait on something, then let it be the stars. I may have a long sit, though, because the stars are afraid to shine over here. I guess somebody told them this is the bad side of town. *(Pause)* Or maybe I'm just waiting for my life to end. Of course, you never can find a carousing fugitive when you need one.

CONSTANCE: Wouldn't suicide be less terrifying than waiting for someone to murder you?

LIZZY *(sarcastically):* Is this a new approach in handling charity cases? Come to think of it, you could save a lot of money if you made euthanasia fashionable for the down-and-out.

CONSTANCE: How can you say such things?

LIZZY: That's strange, I was going to ask you the same question, because I was kidding about wanting to be murdered.

CONSTANCE: That's not a thing to joke about.

LIZZY: Well, isn't comedy better than insanity?

CONSTANCE: Your comments have been much too personal.

LIZZY: Why is it that the rich can pry into the lives of the poor, and it's hailed as concern for humanity, yet if I question your life, I'm rebuked for being offensive? I guess it's because Penniless and Powerless are the aborted twins of society.

CONSTANCE: Aren't we being a bit melodramatic?

LIZZY: What convenient blind spots you people create for yourselves. Tell me, is that an inherited trait, or is that what they teach you in prep school?

CONSTANCE: I'm sorry. I don't mean to make light of your suffering.

LIZZY: Why not? Everybody else does. When I cry, the world just spits on a whimpering fool. Of course, your tears are tended to as if they're pearls of great sadness.

CONSTANCE: I am overlooking your negative comments, because I know—

LIZZY *(interrupting)*: You'll swallow my indignities because I'm one of the "precious beggar pets" that keeps your life full of busyness and your closets full of charity ball gowns.

CONSTANCE: Why are you being so cruel to me?

LIZZY: Hey, maybe I could become one of your before and after posters. "Yes, here she is, one of the swinish masses . . . and now after we've renovated her to make her look more like us." It all makes for such a cozy exchange, doesn't it? You people give us your secondhand clothes and leftover canned goods, and then we absolve you from your decadence.

CONSTANCE *(anger building)*: I have never been talked to like this in my life!

LIZZY: That's because everybody you know weighs the value of truth on the scales of expediency.

CONSTANCE: I don't think I want to hear any more about truth from you. You've already cast the first stone, but the life you live isn't so spotless. Every time you take a handout from anyone, you're saying, "I need help because I'm unable to do anything for myself." I don't see any maimed limbs or mental confusion or lack of education. And here you are. You probably haven't done an honest day's work in your life.

LIZZY: And I suppose you have.

CONSTANCE *(thoughtful pause, then says heavily)*: I thought I had. I'm not sure what I think anymore. Who knows, perhaps we've found common ground. *(Pause, looks at her watch and rises)* I can't imagine what's taking my husband so long. I should have called a taxi. No, I should have told him I'd be waiting in the car, but I hated to do that, because it ran out of gas right in front of a massage parlor. *(Takes some slow, deep breaths to calm herself)* I'm not sure what to do now. I'm running out of time. What do you think I should do?

LIZZY: Why in the world would I care what you do?

CONSTANCE: I don't know. *(Sits back down)* I suppose if you can brave these streets day and night, I can brave them for 30 minutes. (CONSTANCE *hands* LIZZY *her small bag of groceries.)*

LIZZY: What's this for?

CONSTANCE: It's what I drove to the store for. You may have it. And don't bother absolving me from my guilt. I have a fresh supply flown in every month with my caviar.

LIZZY *(takes bag, looks through it, and says sarcastically)*: Oh, this is great . . . a bottle of rotgut liquor, some rubbing alcohol, and three jars of olives. I haven't eaten this good in years. *(Removes bottle of liquor from grocery sack*

18

and looks at it curiously) Excuse me, but is this what stuffed shirts are using for a social lubricant these days? This booze can curl nose hairs.

CONSTANCE: Only the olives were for my guests.

LIZZY *(jokingly):* What's that supposed to mean? This is your hooch? What are you, an alcoholic?

CONSTANCE *(pause, then says seriously):* Yes. I am.

LIZZY *(showing some concern):* Oh. (LIZZY *returns bottle of liquor to sack, pulls out bottle of rubbing alcohol, and says without her earlier enthusiasm for insulting* CONSTANCE.) So the rich use rubbing alcohol for scratches too. You'd better watch out for those nasty cuts, though. If you lose too much of that blue blood, it might affect your livelihood.

CONSTANCE *(turns to* LIZZY *solemnly and says with double meaning):* I'm no longer worried about those nasty cuts. *(Pause)* And that is not what the rubbing alcohol was for.

(Heavy silence)

LIZZY *(a little worried):* Wait a minute. Am I missing something here?

CONSTANCE: You were wrong about "life's helix" being inescapable. There is a way out.

LIZZY: Hey, you're starting to scare me. What is this stuff for?

CONSTANCE: What do you think it's for?

LIZZY *(gradually realizing what* CONSTANCE *means and says with fear):* Your own . . . demise?

CONSTANCE: Funny how *demise* rhymes with *despise.*

LIZZY: Are you kidding? You mean you were really going to chugalug this stuff?

CONSTANCE: I was going to do it earlier in the car when I ran out of gas, but two policemen drove up, and I got frightened. *(Laughs without feeling)* And there I was, stuck in front of that massage parlor, suddenly more worried about losing my good standing in the community than I had been about losing my own life. Tell me, since you're the expert, does that fall under comedy or insanity?

LIZZY *(said uneasily while returning rubbing alcohol to grocery sack):* Why would you want to kill yourself?

CONSTANCE: It's ironic, my husband is a psychiatrist, and he doesn't even know that I drink . . . or perhaps he does know, and he doesn't want me to know he knows. I suppose that game can go back and forth forever . . . like watching your infinite reflection between two mirrors. After a while, nothing seems real.

LIZZY: Why can't you tell your friends and your husband?

CONSTANCE: If I force everybody, including myself, to face who I really am, it's bound to come down to the one thing that some of us can't handle.

LIZZY: What's that?

CONSTANCE: Change.

LIZZY *(sincerely):* All you need is one of those fancy joints where the rich and famous go to dry out.

CONSTANCE: It goes deeper than my drinking. I've got a lifestyle problem. You see, I have more style than I have life. And I'm in a kind of wedlock with charity functions for the needy. You know, till death us do part. Even that would be OK, except our charity members fret more over pedicures than poverty. You have my permission to gloat . . . because you were right. We're not much more than spoiled naughty children, with no one to spank us.

LIZZY: You could do some good if you really wanted to.

CONSTANCE: Perhaps. I'd like to volunteer to be a foster parent, but I'm not sure if my husband is up to it. He can't even handle road noise.

LIZZY: Why are you telling me all this?

CONSTANCE: Because I really did want to hear the truth come out of my mouth . . . even if it was only to a stranger.

LIZZY: So how does truth feel?

CONSTANCE: Like . . . being in the eye of a storm . . . you're grateful for the peace, but fearful of what you know lies ahead.

LIZZY: And what is that?

CONSTANCE: I don't know. Maybe I'll develop an addiction to truth. Who knows, maybe there's even a place for God in all this.

LIZZY *(growing more nervous about the seriousness of the conversation and losing more of her Texas accent):* Does that mean you're going to forget about the rubbing alcohol? You can't kill yourself anyway. Why, that's crazy. You're not crazy . . . are you? Of course you're not.

CONSTANCE: For somebody who's streetwise and shockproof, you're suddenly acting very peculiar about this. I assumed this kind of thing was common on the streets.

LIZZY *(said without really thinking):* Well, people here are usually murdered before they get a chance to commit suicide.

CONSTANCE: That's not what you said earlier. *(Pause)* Are you feeling all right? You're looking rather faint.

LIZZY: I'm OK, but I've got to explain who I really—

CONSTANCE *(interrupting):* Please don't be offended . . . (CONSTANCE *offers her small evening bag to* LIZZY.) But I'd like you to have this.

LIZZY *(accepts evening bag reluctantly, and says without sarcasm):* It is a pretty thing, but I guess I don't have very many outfits to wear it with.

CONSTANCE: You're welcome to take it to a pawnshop. Those aren't rhinestones on the front, they're diamonds. There should be enough cash inside to tide you over until you can sell it. *(Pause)* You know, despite your street manners, or perhaps it's *because* of your street manners, you're more interesting to talk to than most of my friends, and certainly more honest. Maybe we could get together once in a while and just talk, or yell at each other. You know, some people spend whole lifetimes searching, and never finding one person they can trust.

LIZZY *(now completely out of character as a bag lady and with no noticeable accent):* I think I'm getting conversational claustrophobia.

CONSTANCE: And I think I'm getting a little confused. Is your accent fading, or is it my mind?

LIZZY *(honestly):* OK. I'm just going to lay it on you straight. I'm not a bag lady. OK? I'm an actor researching a role as a homeless woman. It's for an upcoming production at the Thorpe Playhouse. (LIZZY *removes tissue from her mesh bag and begins to wipe the dirt off her face.)* The director felt we should not only spend some time with the homeless but try some different approaches with people to sort of expand our vision of the role. Today I was exploring the more cynical side of my character.

CONSTANCE *(trying to hide her pain, because of the deception):* I see. *(Pause)* In that case, you can go back and tell your director that your experiments were very fruitful.

LIZZY *(places small evening bag next to* CONSTANCE): I guess I'd better give this back. *(Pause)* So what are you going to do now?

CONSTANCE *(struggling to present a facade of strength):* I believe I'm going to be hostess at a party in 30 minutes . . . where I will do what all actors do . . . internalize my role and never break character.

LIZZY: If I go, you won't try to kill yourself, or anything like that, will you? I mean, if I ever heard on the news that you'd . . . well, you know, I'd never get over it. The shock of it would probably destroy my acting career.

CONSTANCE: Don't be silly. The crisis has passed. I suddenly realized that I have a full life and a good husband, and I intend on keeping them both.

LIZZY: Well, that's a great relief to me.

CONSTANCE: Earlier you said the eyes tell all. Just out of curiosity, could you really see all those things in me?

LIZZY: Well, usually I make everything up. That's my forte . . . improvisation. But this time it was almost too real. Listen, let me explain something to you. By some coincidence, you have a lot of the same . . . *qualities* as my mother. In fact it's those *qualities* that have kept a war simmering between my mother and me for eons. *(Pause)* But you'll be pleased to know that talking to you today, well, I think it's helped me to finally let it all . . .

CONSTANCE *(finishing her thought):* Boil over?

LIZZY: Yes! Having it out with you was better than five years of therapy.

CONSTANCE: I'm glad I could help you. *(Looks offstage left, still trying to hide her pain)* I think I see one of your colleagues approaching.

(RITA enters SL. She is dressed as a bag lady and is clutching a sack of her belongings while waving an old hat. She is dancing around in circles, acting mentally disturbed.)

RITA *(said almost singing in an eerie high-pitched voice; RITA ends with her hat positioned for a handout):* Hungry spiders from the moon . . . can they survive? Loony spiders from the moon . . . can you spare a five?

LIZZY: Rita, you can take a sanity break now. This woman knows who we are.

RITA *(half-jokingly):* And just when I was on a good roll.

(Uncomfortable silence)

RITA *(to LIZZY):* Well, you might as well introduce us.

LIZZY *(to CONSTANCE):* What was your name again?

CONSTANCE: Constance Rutherford Thorpe.

RITA: You wouldn't by any chance be the same Thorpe that built the new theatre here?

CONSTANCE: That's right.

LIZZY *(to RITA):* What are you talking about?

RITA *(to LIZZY):* Just what I said. It was Mrs. Thorpe here and her husband who donated the money to build the Thorpe Playhouse. *(Condescendingly)* You know, where we are currently working.

LIZZY: Great day!

RITA: You've got that cadaver-white look on your face again, Lizzy. What have you been up to? Wait, let me guess. You've either overbleached your facial hair or you've offended your way out of somebody's favor again.

LIZZY: I'm so embarrassed I think I'm going to throw up.

CONSTANCE: No need for hysterics. I was as impressed with your acting as I was appalled by your insolence. And I'm not even going to have the police arrest you on an I.B.L. . . .

LIZZY: What's that?

CONSTANCE: "Impersonating a Bag Lady."

LIZZY: I know I deserved that . . . and much worse.

CONSTANCE: I suppose we all deserve to be squashed like bugs . . . maybe you more than me.

LIZZY: I hope you won't always remember me as "the hypocrite."

CONSTANCE: Well, it is a tad insincere to mix a sermon on truth with a false identity. But fortunately, truth is still truth, even if the messenger is a . . . an actor . . . and an insensitive twit.

LIZZY (rises): I want to beg your forgiveness for all I've said.

CONSTANCE: You're forgiven, but why didn't you apologize to me before you knew who I was?

LIZZY (worriedly): Oh dear. I guess I've insulted you again.

CONSTANCE (sadly): No, you didn't. But you did remind me just how shallow people can be.

RITA (said while taking LIZZY's arm to go): I think we'd better run along, Lizzy, before you finish digging us six feet under with that enormous shovel you call a mouth.

LIZZY (to CONSTANCE): Would you like me to wait here with you until your husband comes?

CONSTANCE: It's not necessary. He knows exactly where I am, and he'll be here any minute now.

LIZZY: Are you sure?

CONSTANCE: I am sure.

LIZZY (picks up her mesh bag with belongings and says to CONSTANCE): Please, you take care of yourself. OK?

RITA: Bye now.

LIZZY: Bye-bye.

CONSTANCE: Good-bye.

(LIZZY and RITA exit SL. CONSTANCE remains seated on the bench, looks over at the sack of groceries, then reaches for it. She looks around to make sure no one is watching

23

her, and then pulls out the bottle of liquor. CONSTANCE *stares at the full bottle. After a pause, she returns the bottle of liquor to the bag and then pulls out the bottle of rubbing alcohol. She stares at the bottle for a moment, unscrews the lid and considers drinking it. Changing her mind,* CONSTANCE *slowly screws the lid back on the bottle of rubbing alcohol and puts it back into the sack. She pulls out a jar of olives and sets it on the bench.* CONSTANCE *throws all the groceries into the trash bin except for the one jar of olives on the bench. She opens the jar of olives and begins eating them slowly and thoughtfully.* JOHN *enters SR. He is dressed in a tuxedo.)*

JOHN: I came as quickly as I could. It's starting to get dark. Are you all right?

CONSTANCE: Yes, but there is something I need to talk to you about.

JOHN: Don't worry about the car. I'll send somebody out to pick it up.

CONSTANCE: I hadn't even thought about the car.

JOHN: Why are you sitting here eating a jar of olives? Won't that spoil your appetite?

CONSTANCE: I'm not worried about my appetite.

JOHN: I must say, I can't figure any of this out. You insist upon driving to the store right before our party, and then you end up way over here. You could have been mugged . . . or killed. I'm sure you have a lot to tell me, but right now we'd better get home. We have guests arriving in about 25 minutes.

CONSTANCE: John . . . there are some things we need to discuss.

JOHN: You can explain everything at the party.

CONSTANCE: No, I can't. We need to talk now. Natalie can take care of the guests for a while.

JOHN: What is it? You make it sound like life and death.

CONSTANCE: It nearly was.

JOHN: What do you mean? What's going on?

CONSTANCE: Oh, there's a lot going on. In fact, I've kept myself quite busy . . . living with . . . (CONSTANCE *goes to trash can and digs out her sack of groceries and hands it to* JOHN.)

JOHN *(looks in grocery sack and asks with concern):* These are yours?

CONSTANCE: That's right.

JOHN: I don't understand.

CONSTANCE: Well, understanding is a . . . it's a choice . . . that sometimes carries a high price. And I don't know if you're ready to pay it.

JOHN *(pause):* You're right. I don't know if I am.

CONSTANCE: Good. I think those are the first truly honest words that have passed between us.

JOHN *(after a pause, he sits down on bench with* CONSTANCE *and says sincerely):* So, tell me . . . how shall we begin?

Curtain

Caution to the Wind

A Romantic Comedy in One Act

Insider Information

When my husband reads this one-act, he'll chuckle lightly and say, "Sounds a little like our lives. Pretty scary."

Don't let anyone ever tell you that a playwright doesn't sometimes draw deeply from the bountiful well of breakfast table chatter . . . smile.

Cast: One male actor and one female actor

HERSHEL: Hershel and Sylvia are husband and wife. Hershel can be played by a man anywhere from his 20s to 40s. Hershel and Sylvia should be around the same age. Hershel, a geologist, loves his wife very much but has always had difficulty understanding how to express his love through the art of romance.

SYLVIA: Sylvia is an art teacher and more flamboyant in nature than Hershel. Even though she loves Hershel, she longs for him to sweep her off her feet with a little romance.

Scene: We are in the attic of Hershel and Sylvia's home.

Time: It is Saturday afternoon in the present.

Props:

    2 old chairs
    Old boxes
    Trunk
    Pile of old magazines
    Lamp shade (optional)
    Bouquet of plastic roses tied together
    Hat rack
    Tennis racket
    A lady's fan
    A lady's straw hat adorned with flowers and ribbons

Cobwebs

Small clear glass container of dirt (for inside the trunk)

Miscellaneous items for trunk (optional)

Batch of old letters in envelopes with rubber band around them (for inside of trunk)

Other miscellaneous attic junk for effect (optional)

An old man's hat (for inside of trunk)

A partially eaten apple (for Sylvia)

Playing time: 20 to 25 minutes

(In the attic two chairs are set CS. Old boxes are sitting around the chairs as well as an old trunk, magazines, a lamp shade, a bouquet of plastic roses that are tied together, a hat rack, a tennis racket, a woman's fan, and other miscellaneous attic items. Hanging on the hat rack is a woman's old straw hat adorned with flowers and ribbons. A few cobwebs are hanging here and there over the items in the attic. It is Saturday afternoon in the present.

(At rise of curtain, SYLVIA *enters SL, opening and closing an imaginary or framed door.* SYLVIA *is wearing an attractive housedress and is eating an apple as she enters the attic. She moves cautiously as if she hasn't been up in the attic for a long time. She is stooping somewhat at first to give the impression of a slanted ceiling. Once* SYLVIA *reaches CS she is no longer stooping because of the imaginary peak in the roof.)*

SYLVIA *(says in a singsong voice as she anxiously looks around):* OK. It's time for all creepy crawly things to hurry back to their little holes. Shoo, shoo. (SYLVIA *finally begins to relax. She picks up a bouquet of plastic roses, sniffs them, and then says.)* Why am I smelling these? They're plastic.

(She discards the bouquet by nonchalantly throwing it over her shoulder. She puts the partially eaten apple between her teeth while she picks up her old tennis racket and comically swings it around with ridiculous ballet-type movements. She is pretending to hit a tennis ball. She accidentally hits the hat rack and catches it before it falls. She puts the tennis racket down, takes her hat from the hat rack, and puts it on. She takes the apple out of her mouth, picks up a collapsible fan from the top of a box, and fans herself daintily. She sashays about pretending to be a Southern belle and acts out the scene as she says it all aloud with a pretend Southern accent.)

SYLVIA: Blushing profusely, she gazes up at the Baron's tumultuous eyes. His sudden proposal of marriage has stolen her breath away. *(Gasp of air)* She flutters her fan while her dear little heart melts into sunshine. Then in proper Southern fashion, she wilts ever so slightly, pretending to fall into a delicious faint. (SYLVIA *gradually sounds more panicked and uses less and less Southern accent as she becomes more alarmed at the spider crawling on the trunk.)* When suddenly she stops because she sees a large spider on top of the trunk in front of her. *(No longer pretending to be a Southern belle, she yells in a loud and unladylike manner.)* SPIDER! *(No longer using a Southern accent,* SYLVIA *calls out for* HERSHEL, *who is downstairs in the living room reading a magazine.)* Hershel, could you come and kill this spider? Hershel! *(Said with comic fear)* He's coming toward me, and I think he has a gun. Hershel!

(HERSHEL *can be heard offstage left stomping as if he is climbing the attic stairs. He enters SL, through the attic door.* HERSHEL *stoops a bit at first, giving the illusion of a slanted ceiling as he hurries to his wife's aid.)*

HERSHEL: What's all the commotion?

SYLVIA *(pointing to it):* Look. There it is.

HERSHEL: That tiny thing? I thought women weren't scared of spiders anymore.

SYLVIA: That isn't a spider. It's an eight-legged pachyderm! *(Pause)* Look, he's getting away. Why don't you stop him?

HERSHEL: I think I'll let him go on his own recognizance.

SYLVIA: But he has that look of revenge. *(She starts slapping the floor with her shoe, trying to kill the spider. Finally she gives up and stands there looking at the floor.)* Oh . . . he just ran away.

HERSHEL *(comically bland):* Spiders are like that. They have this weird objection to being hammered into puree with a shoe.

SYLVIA: Well, you are just no help at all. Where are all the bison bull he-men to rescue the damsels?

HERSHEL *(plainly):* They've all been driven and herded into male sensitivity conferences.

SYLVIA *(wryly):* Oh, really. *(Still taking small bites of her apple)*

HERSHEL: So, what are you doing up here in the attic anyway?

SYLVIA: I am about to embark upon a splendorous journey into the past via something I am in search of.

HERSHEL *(blandly):* Oh. Well, I'll leave you to it. *(Starts to leave)*

SYLVIA: Wait a minute.

HERSHEL: Yes, dear?

SYLVIA: Aren't you even a teensy bit curious as to what I am searching for?

HERSHEL: Sure. What are you looking for?

SYLVIA: But the point is, you weren't curious until I asked you if you were curious.

HERSHEL: Yes, I suppose I was mildly curious before you asked.

SYLVIA: Then why didn't you ask me what I was looking for?

HERSHEL: Do I have to answer that question?

SYLVIA: Well, in that case maybe I won't tell you.

HERSHEL: OK. You don't have to tell me.

SYLVIA: But I want to tell you.

HERSHEL: Then why don't you?

SYLVIA: I don't know. *(Pause)* Maybe because I not only want to tell you but also need you to really want to know.

HERSHEL: OK. I really, really want to know. Except I think I forgot what it is that I want to know.

SYLVIA: What I was searching for up here.

HERSHEL: Yes . . . that is truly what I really really want to know. Now, will you please tell me what I really want to know so I can go back downstairs and finish my magazine?

SYLVIA: You've still not convinced me you want to know, but I've decided to tell you anyway.

HERSHEL *(comically bland):* I'm thrilled to the point of nausea.

SYLVIA *(frowning a bit from* HERSHEL's *comment):* Well, I am up here looking for our old love letters. You know, the ones we wrote to each other back when we were in college . . . and falling in love.

HERSHEL: Oh, well that's really really nice. I hope you find them. *(Starts to go again and reaches out for the doorknob)*

SYLVIA: But.

HERSHEL *(stands frozen for a moment with his hand still reaching out for the doorknob as he says):* I nearly made it to the door that time. But what, Sylvia?

SYLVIA: Wouldn't you like to help me look for our love letters?

HERSHEL: I'm not going to get out of this one alive, am I?

SYLVIA: That's all right. Please go back to reading your magazine.

HERSHEL: Thank you, dear. *(He starts to leave again.)*

SYLVIA: You can't imagine how excruciatingly tickled I am to please you, dear. I would never want to keep you from something that makes you so happy, when all I have here are letters between a young man and woman who shared their hearts . . . and their love . . . and their life . . . and commitment, and—

HERSHEL (*interrupting her as he opens the trunk to look inside*): Why don't we check in this trunk first?

SYLVIA: That is such a darling thing to say. (SYLVIA *sets her apple down on a box.*)

(*They both rummage around in the truck for a moment.* SYLVIA *pulls out a small clear glass container of dirt.*)

SYLVIA: Oh, look—I found a keepsake.

HERSHEL (*takes the container and looks at it while sitting down in one of the chairs*): It just looks like a bottle full of dirt to me.

SYLVIA (*said sincerely*): It is. But it's also a sweet, symbolic memento of our beginnings. You see, that is a tiny portion of the dust that was under your feet when you asked me out on our first real date to a restaurant.

HERSHEL: Weren't our other dates real?

SYLVIA: I never really counted our first five dates because you just took me to a vending machine and a water fountain.

HERSHEL: Hey, I paid for all of it, didn't I? And as I recall, you ate five Hoggy Cheese Bars and three Cream-Filled Blimp Pies.

SYLVIA: How could you possibly remember that?

HERSHEL: I wrote it all down.

SYLVIA (*thinking he was being sentimental*): Oh, you mean for posterity?

HERSHEL: No, I was trying to take it off my income tax.

SYLVIA: Income tax. How?

HERSHEL: Well, I could write it off as long as I talked about what I was selling.

SYLVIA: So that's why all we ever talked about were super deluxe vacuum cleaners and flexible hose attachments. Oh, oh yeah, and how can I forget our most scintillating, topic . . . nozzle adapter plugs.

HERSHEL: Actually, those were revolving power nozzles.

SYLVIA (*takes the bottle of dirt from* HERSHEL *and says in a disheartened tone*): Well, if *I* was just a tax deduction in college, then *this* is only a bottle full of dirt. (*She drops the bottle dramatically into the trunk.*)

HERSHEL: Now, Sylvie. I really was on a strict budget back then, and selling vacuum cleaners was how I helped put myself through college. And besides, *I* would feel honored to be used as a tax deduction.

SYLVIA: Oh, really.

(HERSHEL *rises and digs into trunk again for the letters.*)

SYLVIA: Hershel, sometimes I think *you* are an alien life form.

HERSHEL (*continues to look in trunk and pretends not to listen to* SYLVIA): That's nice.

SYLVIA: An alien life form who has come from planet ZAR-VAC, where they never listen to their wives.

HERSHEL (*still pretending*): Oh . . . OK.

SYLVIA: An alien life form who is really here to suck up the earth's supply of magazines and transmit all the data using my electric minivac.

HERSHEL (*still pretending not to listen as he looks for letters*): Sure.

SYLVIA: You're no longer listening to me.

HERSHEL: That's because on planet ZAR-VAC we speak only ZAR-MAC. (*He pulls out a batch of letters with a rubber band around them.*) And are these the letters?

SYLVIA: Yes, you found our billets-doux. (*She takes the letters and presses them to her heart with emotion.*)

HERSHEL: Well, I'm glad we found the letters. Enjoy reading them.

SYLVIA: Well, don't you want to read them with me? You know, reminisce a bit?

HERSHEL (*says reluctantly, but sweetly*): Sure. (*He sits down.*)

SYLVIA: Look, here's two from you to me. (*She hands the two letters to him to read.*) And here's two from me to you. Let's see what they say. Isn't this exciting?

HERSHEL: Well, I'd rather be reading my science magazine, but I know this will make you happy, so let's do it.

SYLVIA: Won't this make you happy too?

HERSHEL: No, happiness for me is knowing that the letters are up here safe, and that I am downstairs reading my magazine.

SYLVIA: My darling, you are—

HERSHEL (*interrupting and says methodically*): I already know what you're going to say. I am hiding behind my magazines because I have a psychological need to deny you access to my feelings, because I was raised in an emotionally deprived environment, which has rendered me hopelessly stripped of any and all human sentiment. Is that what you were going to say?

31

SYLVIA: Well, that's the short version.

HERSHEL: I thought so.

SYLVIA: Hershel, you are a man pathetically alone with a pile of periodicals.

HERSHEL: You bet.

SYLVIA *(trying to get a reaction)*: OK. That didn't register, so how about it if I ever so sweetly call you a Cellulose Pinhead.

HERSHEL *(joking back)*: Well, that's a prickly thing to say. Now, can we read a couple of these letters so I can go back downstairs?

SYLVIA *(frustrated)*: Whatever. I know you don't really want to. Do you?

HERSHEL: Sure.

SYLVIA: Well, OK. *(Reads letter a bit dramatically)* This one is from me to you and it begins with "My sweet Hershel. Because of your proposal of marriage, I have not been the same. I feel more alive than I have ever felt, and I wake up to each new day with such hope and joy. I treasure your love, and I look forward to the blessed day of our union. Forever Love from Your Sylvie." *(Touched by her own words)* Isn't that beautiful?

HERSHEL: Sure.

SYLVIA: Look, I've got goose bumps. *(Pause)* Now, Hershel, why don't you read one of your letters to me?

HERSHEL: OK. *(He opens his letter and reads it.)* Let's see . . . my letter says, "Dear Sylvie. Thanks for saying yes that you'll marry me. I am really sorry I couldn't take you to the concert on Friday. I had a really bad case of athlete's foot. But you'll be glad to know that the doctor said it would clear up just as soon as I stopped wearing dirty socks. See you soon. Love, Hershel. P.S. Maybe we could start doing our laundry together, and you could give me some pointers."

SYLVIA *(trying to find something nice about the letter)*: Well . . . that was . . . very . . . nice . . . the way you thanked me for saying yes to your marriage proposal.

HERSHEL: You can't fool me. I know that letter wasn't very . . .

SYLVIA *(finishes his sentence)*: Intimate?

HERSHEL: Right. Well, here, I'll bet this one is better. *(He opens up another letter.)* Wait a minute. This letter isn't from me. *(Says without anger)* It's not in my handwriting. And it's signed, "Yours, Robert." Who's Robert?

SYLVIA: Here, let me see that.

(HERSHEL *hands her the letters.*)

SYLVIA *(looks at the letter for a moment and smiles):* I'm sorry, Hershel. I honestly didn't know I'd saved this. I met Robert in college too. I only dated him for a little while my first year.

HERSHEL: Oh.

SYLVIA: I'll just tear it up if you want me to.

HERSHEL: No you don't have to . . . unless you want to.

SYLVIA: Then I guess I'll keep it . . . just for laughs.

HERSHEL: So what did dear old funny Robert have to say . . . just for laughs.

SYLVIA: You can read the letter if you want to.

(SYLVIA *offers the letter to* HERSHEL. *He looks at it for a moment and then rises from chair and takes it.)*

HERSHEL *(opens the letter and reads it out loud):* Let's see . . . he says, "Dearest Sweetness and Light." *(To* SYLVIA) Didn't he even know your name?

SYLVIA: Yes, of course he did. That is just what he called me. *(She sits down in a chair and listens intently.)*

HERSHEL: Oh. *(Goes back to reading the letter and paces while reading)* Well, anyway, his letter says, "I know not what day it is. You have played my heart-strings, and now I care not what hour has come, except for those we share in tender harmony. Time without you becomes an empty urn, drawing forth the tears of cherubs. But the moment you hasten to my side, the pala-tial gates of paradise flood down their joy through the rejoicing clouds. And it consumes the secret places of my affections. Such rhapsodical bliss is intoxicating like a perfumed nectar. May I dare hope to sup of this sweet drink till I die? Yours into eternity, Robert." (HERSHEL *says sarcastically.)* Well, who does this guy think he is, Robert de Bergerac? Hey, that was pretty funny. Anyway, look at this. He didn't even sign it "Love, Robert."

SYLVIA *(teasing):* He didn't have to.

HERSHEL: I'm glad you didn't date him for very long.

SYLVIA: Why?

HERSHEL: Well, because . . . because . . . well listen to this. He says right here in his letter, "I know not what day it is." (HERSHEL *points to his head and smirks.)* I mean this guy has been up flying with the cherubs without any wings.

SYLVIA: He was a National Merit Scholar and summa cum laude.

HERSHEL: Oh. *(Pause)* Hey, I remember that guy. He was a science major, but he was always protesting any dissecting we did by dressing up as a decapitated frog.

SYLVIA: He was a sensitive young man.

HERSHEL: Sensitive, huh. *(Calmly)* So, you really liked this guy? Why didn't you marry him instead of me?

SYLVIA *(teasing him):* Well, he never asked me.

HERSHEL *(plainly):* You mean if he had asked you, you wouldn't be married to me right now?

SYLVIA: I hadn't even met you then.

HERSHEL *(calmly):* That doesn't answer my question. Well, what if it had been a choice? What if you had known us both at the same time? What if we both had proposed, and then you had to choose?

(SYLVIA *rises and pauses to lightheartedly give* HERSHEL *a hard time.*)

HERSHEL *(sits down):* I guess this is what they call a pregnant pause.

SYLVIA *(sincerely):* Of course I would have married you.

HERSHEL: Hey. I'm not so clodheaded that I can't see you must have been impressed with this guy's flattering flair and oozing . . .

SYLVIA *(finishes his sentence):* Sense of romance?

HERSHEL: Yeah, I guess.

SYLVIA: Yes, he was very romantic, and he had the artist's stroke of genius with his words. But . . . he was very artistic with all the other women on campus too. Later I found out he wrote the same letter to some of the other girls in my dorm. He managed to find intoxicating romance with a *lot* of young women. So, I guess you could say that he summoned not only the tears of cherubs but also tears from half of the girls on campus. He divvied out plenty of cream and sugar, all right. But it was always just to cover a really bad brew.

HERSHEL: So what happened to old Bad Brew Robert?

SYLVIA: Oh, somebody told me he moved out to California. He got some government grant money to test . . . what was it? Oh, yeah, to measure some kind of global effects from cow dung residue.

HERSHEL: Well, hey, I'm glad he found something to do that reflects his character. *(Pause)* Listen, Sylvie . . . I do wish that I could act more . . . I don't know . . . more desperate for you. I guess women like that.

SYLVIA: Women don't need desperate. They just need a little . . . dazzle.

HERSHEL: Dazzle?

SYLVIA *(picks up fan and flutters it in front of her face while speaking):* Yes, it means something sparkling and wonderful and spontaneous. *(Snaps fan shut and darkens her expression)* It does *not* mean recharging leftovers and de-scumming toilets and prying up your soured socks from under the bed and watching the paint peel while you read your magazines hour after hour after hour.

HERSHEL: I have heard of the word *dazzle.*

SYLVIA: Hearing and doing never roost together in this house, Hershel. *(Pause)* You know something, most of the time I wouldn't even need dazzle. Sometimes it would just be nice to know what you're feeling.

HERSHEL: I'm not feeling anything.

SYLVIA: You must be feeling *something!*

HERSHEL: Nothing at all. Well, maybe gas and a blazing sensation in my gut from all those nonstop burritos you give me.

SYLVIA *(occasionally fiddles with objects in the attic as she speaks):* What? That is not true.

HERSHEL: Is so. You have been feeding me double bean burritos with a mountain of yams on the side since the dawn of time.

SYLVIA: Those are healthy foods loaded with nutrients.

HERSHEL: Those burritos are so loaded they work just like an industrial air pump. And your yams are lacking something.

SYLVIA: Lacking what?

HERSHEL: Your yams need a friend who can appreciate them. And I just can't be there for them.

SYLVIA: You *love* yams.

HERSHEL: Watch your language. I consider it a four-letter word.

SYLVIA: Your mother told me they were your favorite veggie.

HERSHEL: When I was a kid I used to give them to our pet rabbit when nobody was looking. He wouldn't eat them, so I tossed them into the toilet. Sometimes it took quite a few flushes to say the final farewell.

SYLVIA: I never dreamed you could be so devious.

HERSHEL: I am pure in every way, except for the yams.

SYLVIA: Well, maybe I could jazz up your yams with curry or cayenne pepper or something.

HERSHEL: Give it up, Sylvia. I would gag on all yams throughout the universe. Yams that were and are and will someday be on someone's unfortunate plate. Yams that disappoint on holidays because everyone expected real potatoes. Yams that conjure up nightmarish images of strange orange root people. Yams that have a name even a mother can hate. Yes, America is on a moral decline because we've been living with the lie of a pretend vegetable.

SYLVIA: And so where have you been throwing *my* yams?

HERSHEL: If I tell you, will you promise not to tell my wife?

SYLVIA: That's a promise that's hard to keep under the circumstances, husband dear.

HERSHEL: If you must know, I mulch your yams into the flowerbed.

SYLVIA (*plops down in a chair*): I don't believe you!

HERSHEL (*rises and moves around the attic, looking at objects*): Sure. That's probably best.

SYLVIA: Oh, really. You know, I had been noticing this intriguing smell as I'm weeding. And it might be interesting to note that every time I smelled that scent in the flowerbed it made me want to quickly whip you up yet another batch of yams. So, I guess those strange orange root people came back to haunt you. What do you think of *them* yams, Hershel?

HERSHEL: I wouldn't know. I am not a thinking or feeling person. Remember? Apparently, I am a blob living in Blobsville consuming more than my fair share of Halloween tubers.

SYLVIA: If you didn't like yams, why did you wait until now to tell me?

HERSHEL: It just seemed easier to hide them.

SYLVIA: So that's why you always went out the backdoor on yam night. I thought it was because my flower garden was so enchanting.

HERSHEL: I *do* like your flower garden.

SYLVIA: Yeah. Especially since it makes a great yam dump.

HERSHEL: Except for those occasional bizarre meals, I would say we have a perfect marriage.

SYLVIA: How can you be so satisfied so easily?

HERSHEL: I don't know. I have everything I need. Life is good. (*Picks up pile of old magazines*) And look. Life just got better. You'll never believe what these beauties are. These were my favorite geology journals. Oh, I can't wait to read these from cover to cover again.

SYLVIA (*sarcastically*): Oh, joy. (*Pause*) Hershel, I honestly want more than this. Life can be so rich and full. Don't you ever notice that we never go anywhere? We never *do* anything. I mean, I want daisies on my bed and a reason to buy mistletoe at Christmas. I want to snuggle in sleeping bags while we watch a desert sunrise. I want us to feed each other chocolate mousse, sing in a snowfall, and carve our initials in a tree. I need you to—

HERSHEL (*interrupting*): Wait a minute. Am I really supposed to do all that stuff?

SYLVIA: No. I had planned on doing all these things with our neighbor, George, down the street.

HERSHEL: That was humor, wasn't it?

SYLVIA: Perhaps I've said enough.

HERSHEL: Yeah, you're right. Maybe you have.

SYLVIA: *Even* on our honeymoon. You didn't *even* take me anywhere dazzling. I mean, Hershel, your honeymoon surprise was taking me on a bus ride to a smelly motel.

HERSHEL: I thought you liked the fragrance of potpourri.

SYLVIA: Only when it's not covered by the stench of rotten garbage just outside our window.

HERSHEL: The motel had character.

SYLVIA: It was so cheap they asked us if we wanted to pay extra for clean towels.

HERSHEL: Yes, but if you will recall, those towels were hand embroidered.

SYLVIA: I'm surprised you could see any of it considering the holes were big enough to put your head through.

HERSHEL: They must have just had a small rodent problem. It can happen in the finest hotels.

SYLVIA: Well, I wouldn't know. I've never been in a fine hotel to see how big their rats are.

HERSHEL: That hotel we stayed at made it right in the end. They didn't even charge us for the honeymoon brunch.

SYLVIA: How could they charge us after we got trapped in *their* rickety elevator for three hours with *their* pet poodle who kept mistaking our new luggage for a fire hydrant.

HERSHEL: The reason we stayed there was because I didn't want us to worry about debts as we were just starting out.

SYLVIA (*rises with emotion*): But just once in a while doesn't a person need to throw caution to the wind?

HERSHEL: People who throw caution to the wind eventually have it fly back in their faces.

SYLVIA (*ignoring his remark*): And while we're talking about *stuff*, I'd like to say that I didn't really like what you bought me for my gift last month.

HERSHEL: Why not?

SYLVIA: Because it was Valentine's Day, and you gave me a gift certificate for an oil lube and filter.

HERSHEL: But at least this year I remembered to gift-wrap your present. Don't I get some kudos for that?

SYLVIA: Not when you gift-wrap it with the paper off my pork chops.

HERSHEL: I was hoping you hadn't noticed that.

SYLVIA: And the ribbon you tied it up with . . . it looked like you'd dug it out of the trash.

(HERSHEL *sits down and tries not to look guilty.*)

SYLVIA: You are kidding?

HERSHEL: Remember our vows . . . till death us do part.

SYLVIA *(lightly exasperated):* You're hopeless. Here I am brimming with effervescent life bubbles and you're busy blamoing them with your little popgun. *(Softening)* Oh, it's all right about the gift. And I know I should forget the past. But . . . it's just that there were so many things I wanted to experience with you. I mean, I thought that was one of the reasons we got married.

HERSHEL: I married you because I love you.

SYLVIA: But doing things together *comes* from loving.

HERSHEL: We *do* things. Don't we? *(Rises and looks in trunk again)*

SYLVIA: Going shopping for new car tires and weather stripping for the house just doesn't count.

HERSHEL: But we're together. And we're doing things that are important maintenance for our car and home. Sure it counts.

SYLVIA: Listen to yourself, Hershel. It's pathetic and beyond.

HERSHEL *(notices his old hat in the trunk and puts it on):* Look, it's my wild plum picking hat.

SYLVIA: You're changing the subject because you don't want to deal with the possibility that *you* are wrong, and I am—

HERSHEL *(interrupting):* I think that about covers it. You know, I used to pick wild plums near our creek. And I always wore this hat. Mother liked to make it into jam. Lots and lots of jam.

SYLVIA: And did you flush her *jam* down the toilet too? It rhymes with *yam* after all.

HERSHEL: No. I loved her jam. *(Referring to SYLVIA)* There *are* things I love.

SYLVIA: Well, it's just hard to tell sometimes. *(Softening a bit)* You know that was very thoughtful of you to pick wild plums for your mother. I suppose if I strain a bit, I could put thoughtful under a romantic heading.

HERSHEL: *That's* my Sylvie.

SYLVIA: Not so fast. You're not off the hook so easily.

HERSHEL: Hey, I'm a reasonable kind of guy. What if we do something that you think is romantic . . . say . . . twice a year.

SYLVIA: Twice a year? I shouldn't even speak to you after that offer. *(Pause)* Once a month minimum.

HERSHEL: I always love the way you negotiate. OK. It's a deal.

SYLVIA: I guess that means the rest of the month you'll read your mags. Right?

HERSHEL: Reading is thrilling to me. It teaches me new things. It's fascinating, up-lifting, mind-opening. It's really exciting when I get a brand-new magazine. Even the smell of it. *(Takes in a deep breath)* New mags have this really great scent. Then I flip through it quickly at first just to see what's to come. That's another great part of the whole process. Of course, then there are those long, wonderful hours that I can digest all that valuable information. It's just so—

SYLVIA *(interrupting with anger building)*: Excuse me. I knew you loved reading. But perhaps it's really a consuming *passion*. I'm grateful that you feel this. I am happy for you that you have such a glorious hobby. I celebrate and rejoice with you in your pleasure. But I just wish I could have an *ounce* of that interest and fervor for me! I mean, I can't believe my *life* and *love* and *feelings* are all being upstaged by a stack of processed wood pulp!

HERSHEL *(sits down and looks at her seriously)*: I guess you really do mean all this, don't you?

SYLVIA *(solemnly)*: Yes. I do.

HERSHEL: Why did you wait until now to tell me?

SYLVIA: It's not like the yams. I haven't been hiding *myself* from *you*. All of these things have been said over and over, until *you* can even spout them with-out really hearing it! But you're like a radio that's tuned into some foreign station. I can never really reach you.

HERSHEL *(sincerely)*: Well. I'm listening now. *(Pause)* So . . . do you ever think about . . . him?

SYLVIA: Who? Oh, you mean Robert?

HERSHEL: Yes.

SYLVIA: Sometimes. But I'm glad nothing came of it. He would have made me very unhappy.

HERSHEL: Well, it appears I'm not doing much better.

SYLVIA: Well . . .

HERSHEL: Well what?

SYLVIA: You're a mess. That's true. But . . .

HERSHEL: But?

SYLVIA: I do love you, and you are so uniquely helpful.

HERSHEL: I've heard helpful is good.

SYLVIA *(genuinely):* Like when I feel so suffocated by life's debris, you have this way of helping me breathe again. Just you being there comforts me.

HERSHEL: I'm glad. *(Pause)* You know, I do wish I could get my mind to work romantically for you. Maybe you could give me some pointers like you did in college.

SYLVIA: You mean like the laundry pointers?

HERSHEL: Yeah. Like that.

SYLVIA *(gently):* OK. But romance isn't like following a manual. It's something that flows from the heart.

HERSHEL: I guess I've always been a manual kind of a guy. *(Thoughtful pause)* I honestly don't know if I can change a lot. But I have taken you for granted. And that makes me sad.

SYLVIA: Really?

HERSHEL: You know, I won't forget my promise about us doing something together once a month. I *am* good at keeping promises.

SYLVIA: Yes, you are.

HERSHEL: I *do* love you, and I am committed to you.

SYLVIA *(sincerely):* Thank you for saying that, Hershel.

HERSHEL *(rises and says lightly):* By the way, have I ever told you I think I can carry you downstairs without getting a hernia?

SYLVIA: No. I can honestly say you have never said that to me. But maybe we could just hold hands going downstairs. You know, part of doing things romantically means you have to be alive to enjoy them.

HERSHEL: Are you saying I can't lift you?

SYLVIA: I tell you what, after we walk downstairs, you can carry me to the couch.

HERSHEL: So we can snuggle next to the fireplace. See, I'm getting the hang of this thing. Soft music to swoon by. And lots and lots of candles.

SYLVIA: Plenty of light so you can read your magazines?

HERSHEL: No. So, I can see your lovely face while we share our feelings.

SYLVIA: I thought you said you didn't feel *anything*.

HERSHEL: Men feel lots of things. Sometimes it just takes a few hours to chisel it off of us. We're just wired differently than women. And that's good. *(Trying to say it romantically)* 'Cause I really love the way you're wired.

SYLVIA *(sincerely)*: Why, Hershel, I think that's the most romantic thing you have ever said to me.

HERSHEL: Yes, it was. And how about we throw some caution to the wind and go on a real honeymoon? We can afford it now.

SYLVIA: Really? That is such a darling thing to say.

HERSHEL *(pleased with himself)*: Yes, it is.

SYLVIA: Could we go to an exotic beach or to the mountains?

HERSHEL: Yes. We can go anywhere they don't serve yams. And we can even fly.

SYLVIA: Wait a minute. Will you be taking your magazines along on our second honeymoon?

HERSHEL *(teasingly)*: Absolutely not. I'm sure the hotel will have more than enough.

SYLVIA *(lightheartedly)*: Ohhh. *(She pulls the hat down over* HERSHEL*'s eyes.)*

HERSHEL *(humorously)*: Just kidding. Just kidding.

(They laugh together. SYLVIA *lifts his hat back up. They look at each other romantically. The light fades to a blackout as they come together for a warm embrace.)*

Curtain

No Place to Scream

A Drama/Comedy in One Act

Insider Information

I have never known a hermit personally, but on occasion I've felt like a good scream was in order. This is part of what our heroine is searching for in *No Place to Scream*.

Also, this one-act is about truth being forced from its hiding place, which is still at the top of my list of all-time favorite themes.

Cast: One male actor and one female actor

SERAPHINA: An intelligent, middle-aged, single woman who is a former owner of a chain of flower shops. She has been hurt deeply by her career, family, and friends. Seraphina desires to reach out for love and happiness again, but just hasn't had the courage to leave her solitary life. She sees a special spark in Franklin that warms her. He also awakens her desire to consider leaving her hermit lifestyle and begin really living again.

FRANKLIN: An intelligent, middle-aged, single man who owns his own computer business. He is somewhat bland in nature but has a spark that seems to flicker brightly around Seraphina. His fiancé has never been able to see or enhance that spark. Franklin and Anne were marrying more out of fear of growing old alone than of a real love for each other.

Scene: We are on the rundown porch of Seraphina's shack in the middle of a forest in eastern Oklahoma.

Time: It is springtime on a Saturday morning in the present.

Props:

> General: Old outdoor glider
>> Old coffee table
>> Old rocking chair
>> Old pots
>> Large jars of wildflowers (could be silk)

Colored bottles
Tools
Buckets
"Beware of Dog" painted on an old board
Bowl of blackberries
Basket of cornbread covered with cloth
Pitcher of water
Cup
Other miscellaneous junk for porch (optional)

Seraphina: Shabby sweater
Book
Rubber band for hair

Franklin: Watch
Wallet
Wad of cash in wallet

No special sound effects or lighting required.

Playing time: 30 minutes

(We are on the rundown porch of SERAPHINA's shack in the middle of a forest in east-ern Oklahoma. A dilapidated outdoor glider, coffee table, and rocking chair are sitting CS. The walls and floor of the porch can be illusionary. Large jars of wildflowers are sitting on the coffee table, floor, etc. Old pots, colored bottles, tools, buckets, and other miscellaneous items are sitting on the porch. Also, the words "Beware of Dog" are painted on a board, which is sitting next to SERAPHINA's glider. A bowl of blackberries, a basket of cornbread, a pitcher of water, and a cup are also sitting on the coffee table. SERAPHINA is a middle-aged, single woman, who has retreated from life to live as a her-mit for the last five years. She is wearing a plain dress and a shabby sweater. Her hair is tied back, and she is wearing no makeup and no shoes. It is springtime on a Satur-day morning in the present.

(As the curtain rises, SERAPHINA is sitting on the glider reading a book. She is humming a tune softly as she swings gently on the glider. There is a pause and then suddenly a man named FRANKLIN enters SL in a hurry and out of breath. FRANKLIN is a middle-aged, single man who has lost his way on the dusty and forested back roads of eastern Oklahoma. His car has run out of gas, and he has walked about two miles try-ing to find help. FRANKLIN is wearing a very nice suit and is very well-groomed, ex-cept for his dusty shoes.)

FRANKLIN (out of breath): Oh, I'm so glad I've found you. I mean . . . somebody
. . . anybody.

SERAPHINA (*a bit alarmed*): Who are you? (*She puts her book down, picks up her "Beware of Dog" sign, and then holds it in front of herself.*) I got a killer dog, and he likes to eat city folk.

FRANKLIN (*concerned*): Wait a minute. I'm living a somewhat meaningful life, and I want to finish it. Please.

SERAPHINA: I done asked you a question.

FRANKLIN: I forgot what it was.

SERAPHINA: Who are you?

FRANKLIN: Franklin Edwards. I'm harmless. I have a subdued personality because I work with computers. I don't hunt small animals, tell unseemly jokes, . . . or . . . or watch violent sports. Does that make you feel better?

SERAPHINA: No. I hate comedians.

FRANKLIN: Believe me. I don't have the capacity. At least certainly not today.

SERAPHINA: What are you doing up here on my land? Ain't nobody comes up here.

FRANKLIN: I got lost on some back road and then my car ran out of gas and then . . . I thought I saw a light through the trees up here.

SERAPHINA: I ain't got no lights. It was the sun on my weather vane.

FRANKLIN: Well, anyway, I need to use a phone. My cellular one seems to be on the blink. I'm in a hurry.

SERAPHINA: Good. You can hurry yourself right back to where you came from. Now get off my property.

FRANKLIN: That's the point. I can't. As I said, my car has run out of gas. I've got my fiancé waiting for me right now at the Wendell Estate. (*He looks at his watch.*) I was supposed to announce our engagement an hour ago at a party. I have to call her . . . or . . . or I could lose my life.

SERAPHINA: You mean she's going to kill you?

FRANKLIN: Only metaphorically . . . but somehow that's worse than the real thing.

SERAPHINA: Well, I could call out my dog and we could find out which is worse.

FRANKLIN (*plainly*): Won't you please let me use your telephone? Then I promise I will get off your land forever.

SERAPHINA: I ain't got no telephone.

FRANKLIN: What do you mean?

SERAPHINA: Can't you understand English?

FRANKLIN: Yes, of course, I majored in it. I just never heard of anyone who didn't have a telephone. It is a standard piece of civilization.

SERAPHINA: Are you saying I ain't civilized?

FRANKLIN: No . . . well maybe. Look, I don't have time for an argument. I've got to get to a telephone. Do you have any neighbors?

SERAPHINA: I suppose there are a few people around here somewhere . . . but I ain't never paid no attention to them.

FRANKLIN: Do you have a car? I'll buy it from you. You look like you could use some money. *(He reaches in his pocket for his wallet and starts to take out a large amount of cash.)*

SERAPHINA: Put your money away. I ain't got no car neither.

FRANKLIN: This is bizarre. Everybody has a car.

SERAPHINA: You know, since you've been here, you've called me uncivilized, dirt poor, and a liar. You sure got yourself a pretty loose tongue for somebody who is about to be eaten alive by a thick-necked dog who hates city folk.

FRANKLIN: I am very sorry. I don't want to be here. I want nothing more than to leave this place. But I need your help. At least tell me where the nearest town is. Surely you must go into town.

SERAPHINA: After you walk back down *my* hill, there's a dirt road. *(Points SR)* Down that dirt road is a place called Fork in the Road. There's a building there. They sell food and supplies.

FRANKLIN: Supplies? What is this . . . the wild west?

SERAPHINA: Are you laughing at me again?

FRANKLIN: No . . . no.

SERAPHINA: Good. Well, you'd better get.

FRANKLIN: Well, how far is this store down the road?

SERAPHINA: Two miles.

FRANKLIN *(shocked):* Two miles! With these hills, it might take me another hour of walking.

SERAPHINA: In them silly shoes you got on, it may take you all day.

FRANKLIN: Does the store have a telephone?

SERAPHINA: Course it does. It doesn't work most of the time, but they got one.

FRANKLIN: What do you mean their telephone doesn't work most of the time?

SERAPHINA: I don't know much about it. I only go there a few times a year for supplies.

FRANKLIN: I've already hiked two miles. I don't want to hike another two miles to find a telephone that's out of order.

SERAPHINA: You better get. I see a storm brewing over there. Then you're going to be slipping in mud for two miles. Them roads gets deep in mud.

FRANKLIN: I'm left with no choice. I am against the wall. This is turning out to be the worst day of my life.

SERAPHINA: No, it could have been worse.

FRANKLIN: How?

SERAPHINA: I could have had a shotgun instead of a dog.

FRANKLIN (lightly sarcastic): That's very amusing.

SERAPHINA: You'd better get.

FRANKLIN: Yes . . . I'd better go. The clouds are looking rather ominous over there. Well, good-bye. (He exits SR.)

SERAPHINA (the moment FRANKLIN exits, she starts to call after him, first softly, then gradually more loudly): Stranger. Hey . . . stranger man. Hey . . . you.

FRANKLIN (after a pause, enters SR): What's going on? I thought you were desperate to be rid of me.

SERAPHINA: I am.

FRANKLIN: Then what are we doing?

SERAPHINA: That store.

FRANKLIN: Yes?

SERAPHINA: It ain't open today. It's Saturday.

FRANKLIN: What?

SERAPHINA: It won't open again until Monday morning.

FRANKLIN: Oh . . . yea. You mean you were going to have me walk two miles in the mud to finally find out that the place that may or may not have a working phone is really closed?

SERAPHINA: Seems like I done you kind of dirty, doesn't it? (She starts to chuckle.)

FRANKLIN: Yes . . . it does seem that way. What am I supposed to do now? Walk around in the forest until Monday?

SERAPHINA: Sure does seem that way.

FRANKLIN: You know, I have always heard about country hospitality.

SERAPHINA: Is that right?

FRANKLIN: But so far I've only heard about it.

SERAPHINA: I know you're sniffing around for an invite to this fine porch, but . . .

FRANKLIN: But . . . what?

SERAPHINA: Listen, the sheriff is coming to check on me and bring me some planting seeds. Well, you finally got a way out, 'cause he's due up to my hill this afternoon. So if you wait by the road down there, he'll see you and take you where you got to get to.

FRANKLIN: Why didn't you tell me this before?

SERAPHINA: It don't matter. I'm telling you now.

FRANKLIN: I hate to dampen your most generous offer, but this afternoon is a long time. I'm not thrilled about hours of sitting in the mud.

SERAPHINA: Balderdash! Ain't you city folks picky?

FRANKLIN: Yes, that's probably true.

SERAPHINA: Why don't you just go back to your car?

FRANKLIN: That's a two-mile hike away. And what if the sheriff comes from the other direction? I'll miss him entirely. And then I'll be back here anxiously awaiting some more of your welcoming spirit and gracious help.

SERAPHINA: Well, what do you want me to do?

FRANKLIN: Never mind. (*He starts to go.*)

SERAPHINA: Oh stop your yapping and sit down.

FRANKLIN (*offended*): I do not . . . yap.

SERAPHINA: Oh, yes you do. You city folks do so much straining on bulky words, I'm surprised you all don't give yourselves verbal hernias. Oh, hooey. Why don't you just sit down?

FRANKLIN: What about your dog? Is he feeling good about me sitting down too?

SERAPHINA: I ain't got no dog.

FRANKLIN: You must really enjoy lying with such free abandon.

SERAPHINA: Tarnation! What are you bellyaching for? You've been invited to sit down. The next thing you know, you'll be pestering me for something to drink.

FRANKLIN (*starts to leave and says plainly*): Excuse me, but in your own vernacular, *you,* lady are a pack of lies and a heap of trouble. And I'm a-thinking that a sit in the mud for five hours is a sight better than five minutes of that thrashing machine you call a mouth.

SERAPHINA: Well, the boy from the city has got some teeth. And here I thought all you could do was gum those fancy little words of yours like a baby eating mush.

FRANKLIN: Yeah, well I didn't know I had any teeth either. But if you'll excuse me . . . the mud awaits.

SERAPHINA: Oh, come on now. Don't be barking too loudly. You'll make me think you don't like me.

FRANKLIN: I don't.

SERAPHINA: Well, if you sit down . . . I'll even bring you a drink of some water from my spring.

FRANKLIN: Well . . . maybe. Why are you suddenly being so nice to me? (*Lightly*) You're not planning on shooting me for target practice . . . are you?

SERAPHINA: Not if I can help it. (*She starts to chuckle in a friendly manner.*)

FRANKLIN (*he chuckles with her*): I shouldn't be laughing.

SERAPHINA: Why not? (*She pours him a cup of water from the pitcher sitting on the outdoor coffee table.*)

FRANKLIN (*he sits down on the rocking chair*): Because my life ends today . . . at least a significant part of it.

SERAPHINA: You sure don't look too forlorn about it.

FRANKLIN: I am desperately forlorn.

SERAPHINA: Then how come your shoulders are so straight and your eyebrows are so peaceful looking?

FRANKLIN: You don't even know me, and up until about two minutes ago you were about to unleash a man-eating dog on me that doesn't exist, which doesn't count because if you had a foaming-at-the-mouth dog you would have let him chew me up, so . . .

SERAPHINA: So what's your point?

FRANKLIN (*trying to convince her and himself*): I am desperately forlorn.

SERAPHINA: I am good enough a woman to let you believe that if you are needing to believe it that much.

FRANKLIN: Well, I'm not sure I like the way you worded that, but I am good enough a man to let it go.

SERAPHINA: Well, ain't that fine?

FRANKLIN: It appears so.

SERAPHINA: Well, all your forlorn fretting is probably for nothing, 'cause before long nobody will even remember this day happened. She'll forget and you'll forget, and if you do ever remember just a little of this, it will be just enough for you two to laugh and kiss about.

FRANKLIN: I like the way that sounds, but then you don't know my fiancé.

SERAPHINA: What's the matter with her?

FRANKLIN: She's very refined and . . . organized . . . but . . .

SERAPHINA: It's always those little buts that get you.

FRANKLIN: Let's just say that her forgiving is more celebrated than her forgetting. But it's difficult for me to be too hard on her. She has put up with a lot from me, I'm sure. At least that's what she says. I am somewhat bland, you see. I guess bland isn't always a treat for those with a discerning life palate. But then . . . she and I aren't getting any younger.

SERAPHINA: True, but you're going to feel a whole lot older a whole lot faster if you marry the wrong woman just because you feel desperate and forlorn about growing old.

FRANKLIN: I think you're twisting my words.

SERAPHINA: I think I'll just shut my trap up before I get my foot caught in it.

(They both sit there in silence for a moment with SERAPHINA *gliding and* FRANKLIN *rocking.)*

FRANKLIN: So what time exactly is the sheriff coming?

SERAPHINA: Whenever the sun hits the tops of them trees over there.

FRANKLIN: But what time is that?

SERAPHINA: I don't know.

FRANKLIN: You don't have a clock?

SERAPHINA: No.

FRANKLIN: Would you . . . like . . . a clock?

SERAPHINA: No.

FRANKLIN: Do you mind if I ask why?

SERAPHINA: What do I need one for?

FRANKLIN: Please excuse my curiosity, but you really have no telephone, car, or electricity?

SERAPHINA: Ain't got none of those things.

FRANKLIN: I've never known anyone like you.

SERAPHINA: And you still don't . . . know me.

FRANKLIN: No, I don't suppose I do. But I mean I've never met anyone that didn't have the basic elements of . . . you know . . .

SERAPHINA: Gadgets don't civilize humanity. Look over there. *(She points to the sky.)*

FRANKLIN: What is it?

SERAPHINA: I don't hear any thunder, but part of the sky is turning that strange green color.

FRANKLIN: What does that mean?

SERAPHINA: It means that something's coming.

FRANKLIN: What is coming?

SERAPHINA: I don't know, but the last time the sky looked like that, I nearly lost my house in a storm. The winds got up, and I never heard such howling sounds in all my born days. It was like the wind and the forest was crying out for something.

FRANKLIN: Aren't you afraid to live up here by yourself?

SERAPHINA *(pause):* Sometimes.

FRANKLIN: Then may I ask why you do it?

SERAPHINA: You may ask it, but I may not answer it.

FRANKLIN: That's fair enough.

SERAPHINA: I think you look like you're hungry. I just picked some wild blackberries this morning. Would you like some?

FRANKLIN: Wild blackberries. I don't think I've ever eaten any . . . wild anyway.

SERAPHINA: They're very good. Try one. *(She takes a handful and gently offers them to him.)*

FRANKLIN *(takes one from her hands and smells the aroma of it, then eats it slowly and thoughtfully):* It's good.

SERAPHINA: Please have some more, if you'd like. *(She offers him the bowl, and he accepts it.)*

FRANKLIN: Thank you. *(He slowly eats the blackberries as they visit.)*

SERAPHINA: But you don't want to eat *too* many wild blackberries.

FRANKLIN: Why not?

SERAPHINA: Because you might grow to love them too much.

FRANKLIN: What would that matter?

SERAPHINA: Well, once I heard tell of a farmer man, who lived in these parts many years ago, and who ate so many of his wild blackberries, he began to think of nothing else. *(She gradually loses her backwoods vernacular.)* But finally the berries on his land didn't satisfy him anymore, so he crossed over the fence and tasted the berries on the other side. They were sweeter than he had ever imagined. While he was picking some more berries, the owner of the land saw him. He looked up from his thievery and was surprised to discover the new landowner was a lovely woman. She was very generous and took baskets of her berries over to the farmer, because she knew how much he loved them. And they would talk and laugh together for hours while they feasted on his coffee and her wild blackberry pie.

FRANKLIN *(failing at his attempt to hide his interest in the ending of the story):* So . . . is that it? Is that all of the story?

SERAPHINA: No.

FRANKLIN: What happened to them?

SERAPHINA: Well, the farmer couldn't get over the fact that the berries were hers to share and not his to own, so one day he took all he had saved in his lifetime and demanded that she sell him the land. Well, she did sell it to him and went away desperately sad, because she had grown to love the farmer very much.

FRANKLIN: I'll bet I know the ending. The farmer discovered the berries were sour after all.

SERAPHINA: No. Just the opposite. The berries seemed to be sweeter than ever. And it made the farmer desperately sad too, because now the berries reminded him of the woman. And he realized that he loved her. But it was too late.

FRANKLIN: Didn't he know where she'd gone?

SERAPHINA: He was so preoccupied with his treasure that he let her leave without finding out where she was going. And so the real jewel of his life slipped away, forever. And even when the ripe fruit was hanging heavy on the vines, the farmer could never again eat another wild blackberry.

FRANKLIN *(sadly sets the bowl of blackberries on the table):* I am suddenly not very hungry for blackberries. So, I suppose the moral to this story is . . . there is a heavy price to be paid for our obsessions.

(SERAPHINA *is silent.*)

FRANKLIN: So . . . is the woman in the story . . . is it . . .

SERAPHINA: Is it what?

FRANKLIN: Is it . . . you?

SERAPHINA: Well, I don't think it can be, because I'm still here. *(Smiling)* At least I think I am.

FRANKLIN: You know, you've never told me your name.

SERAPHINA: I know.

FRANKLIN: I told you *my* name.

SERAPHINA: I've already forgotten it.

FRANKLIN: That doesn't count, and *you* are being secretive.

SERAPHINA: Well, I'm supposed to be secretive. I'm a hermit.

FRANKLIN: Is that what you really are?

SERAPHINA: Isn't that what you think I am?

FRANKLIN: Not really.

SERAPHINA: Why not?

FRANKLIN: Well, for one thing, your backwoods dialect or accent or whatever it is keeps curiously coming and going. *(Smiling at her)* And I *ain't* quite been able to figure out why . . . yet.

SERAPHINA: If I'm not a hermit, then what am I? I've been wondering for years.

FRANKLIN: Do you really want to know what I think?

SERAPHINA *(without anger):* Not really, but you're stuck on my porch for hours, so I suppose I'm forced to know, whether I want to or not.

FRANKLIN: Well, I won't tell you then.

SERAPHINA: The less said . . . the better.

(They are both silent for a moment.)

SERAPHINA *(picks up basket of cornbread on coffee table, folds back the cloth, and offers some to FRANKLIN):* Men would usually rather eat than talk. Maybe you'd rather have something else to eat.

FRANKLIN: I'm not just any man.

SERAPHINA: Is that right? *(She sets basket down on the table.)* Well, you're still welcome to some of my homemade cornbread.

FRANKLIN: Thank you. I will. *(He takes a piece and eats a bite of it.)* You're not going to tell me a sad tale about the cornbread now, are you?

SERAPHINA: No. Cornbread is too ordinary to link itself to such a desperate romance. *(She occasionally munches on cornbread and blackberries.)*

FRANKLIN: I don't think there is anything ordinary about your cornbread. It's wonderful. *(Continues to eat cornbread)*

SERAPHINA: Thank you.

FRANKLIN: I also noticed you keep using the word *desperate*.

SERAPHINA: Yes, I do.

FRANKLIN: You don't think I am?

SERAPHINA: I think you are desperate . . . but . . .

FRANKLIN: But what?

SERAPHINA: I shouldn't be commenting on your affairs. I don't even know you.

FRANKLIN: I'm giving you permission to meddle. Maybe what I need is a fresh perspective.

SERAPHINA: Then I believe you are a man who was desperate to take a wrong turn and get lost in the woods.

FRANKLIN: You mean to avoid announcing my engagement.

SERAPHINA: I don't really know. It was just a feeling. Don't take me too seriously. It would be foolish to change your whole life just because of what some stranger in the woods felt for a fleeting moment.

FRANKLIN: Well, we wouldn't be strangers if you told me your name.

SERAPHINA: I can't figure out why it matters to you.

FRANKLIN: I can't figure out why it does either.

SERAPHINA: You're only interested because I won't tell you. Men are attracted to mystery. They can't help it. It's a malfunction in one of their brain hemispheres.

FRANKLIN: You certainly seem to be an expert on men for someone who rarely ever sees one.

SERAPHINA: There's not much to know. And just to calm your hemisphere . . . my name is . . . Seraphina.

FRANKLIN: Seraphina. I've never known anyone with that name. It makes me think of Seraphim . . . you know—angels.

SERAPHINA: My mother named me after them.

FRANKLIN: It's beautiful.

SERAPHINA: So are the clouds up there. Look at them whirl. My mother always said they were really cherubs dancing in pretty white gowns. But then every mother who ever lived has something to say about angels.

FRANKLIN: Funny, I don't even remember my mother mentioning them. I don't think she ever thinks about angels.

SERAPHINA *(removes her band, letting her hair fall down)*: She doesn't?

FRANKLIN: No. *(Pause)* Where is your mother now?

SERAPHINA *(wistfully)*: She's up there dancing with the cherubs.

FRANKLIN: Oh.

SERAPHINA: What about you? Where's your mother?

FRANKLIN: She's at the party. So is my father. And Anne's father and her mother and every friend she's ever had since the womb. Except me. By now they're thinking . . . I don't know what they're thinking. They must hate me for not showing up. They're mumbling how unworthy I am of her. They're right. But then again, maybe they'll have the police out looking for me thinking I got stranded somewhere.

SERAPHINA: And what do you *hope* they are thinking and doing?

FRANKLIN: I hope . . .

SERAPHINA: Don't you know?

FRANKLIN: No, I don't know.

SERAPHINA: Don't you love her?

FRANKLIN *(rises and moves around the porch, looking at the items on her porch)*: I love some things . . . *about* her.

SERAPHINA: I don't think that's the same.

FRANKLIN: So you're an expert on love too?

SERAPHINA: No.

FRANKLIN: Have you ever been in love?

SERAPHINA: Listen, I don't want to . . . I have something I should tell you, but it's not about love. I have some . . . gasoline.

FRANKLIN: What? I thought you said you didn't have a car?

SERAPHINA: I don't have a car . . . but I have some . . . gasoline.

FRANKLIN: Well, why didn't you tell me that earlier? I would have paid you generously.

SERAPHINA: I already told you. I don't want your money.

FRANKLIN: Well, what is it you want from me?

SERAPHINA: What makes you think I want something from *you?*

FRANKLIN: Well, earlier you were desperate to get rid of me. This was your chance. The gasoline would have done that. I would have been gone. You must want something from me to keep me here.

SERAPHINA: You certainly are assuming a lot of things.

FRANKLIN: I'm just calling it like I see it.

SERAPHINA: Oh, yeah, what else do you see?

FRANKLIN: I see a lonely . . . and lovely woman . . . who is hiding from something.

SERAPHINA *(rises):* Let me get that gasoline for you.

FRANKLIN: Don't bother.

SERAPHINA: Why not?

FRANKLIN: I don't want to go just yet.

SERAPHINA: Why not?

FRANKLIN: Because it's too late to go to the party. It's too late to make her understand I can't live without her. But then . . . why does that sound so foreign?

SERAPHINA: What?

FRANKLIN *(said with revelation as he sits back down on the rocking chair):* Because I *can* live without her. And she will be much happier with someone else. *(Pause)* I just said something I didn't think I'd ever say . . . out loud.

SERAPHINA: Is it the truth?

FRANKLIN: It just sort of popped out.

SERAPHINA: Search your heart.

FRANKLIN: I think that's a female thing. I don't really know how to do that.

SERAPHINA: Well, hiding things certainly doesn't seem to be gender-related.

FRANKLIN: So, I'm hiding truth from myself?

SERAPHINA *(ignoring his question):* You know, you're really not that old.

FRANKLIN: Why do you say *that?*

SERAPHINA: Because you said you weren't getting any younger.

FRANKLIN: I will overlook the fact that you didn't answer my question. *(Pause)* Well, these last several years . . . for some reason I have felt old. I felt like my life was . . . well that was what I loved about Anne.

SERAPHINA: She made you feel young again?

FRANKLIN: Yes. And I just up and decided one day, it was time I got married. She was the person I was dating, and so I sort of . . . forced myself to fall in love with her.

SERAPHINA *(sits back down on the glider):* You can do that?

FRANKLIN: I thought I had. We were to be married right away, so we'd have time to start a family. We had it all planned out. Even how the kids would be spaced and where they'd go to college. Everything. And then I was driving down this country road . . . and this fear came through me. I wondered if . . . after our years had been feverishly spent, and we'd met all of our lists and goals, if we'd look at each other and wonder why we did it all. I had it so wrapped up in my mind . . . perfectly . . . but I guess my heart was feeling something else.

SERAPHINA: You can't go against your heart. Well, you can . . . but if you do . . . well . . .

FRANKLIN: What are *you* hiding from . . . Seraphina?

SERAPHINA *(ignoring his question):* Did you hear that?

FRANKLIN: What was it? Thunder?

(SERAPHINA *rises. They both listen intently for a moment.)*

FRANKLIN: I don't hear anything . . . except our breathing. It is so peaceful here. I forgot what real quiet was. I think I like it. Is that why you came here?

SERAPHINA *(ignoring his question):* Rats.

FRANKLIN: You came here for the rats?

SERAPHINA: No. I'm disgusted by them. The filthy things run under my porch. I can hear them. I have never been able to get rid of them. Sometimes I think they've come just to spite me.

FRANKLIN: Well, as long as they stay under there and you're up here, why does it bother you? I mean, you've put up with worse. You don't even have electricity or a phone, for goodness' sake. What are a few rodents compared to those inconveniences?

SERAPHINA: Because rats infect and destroy what is good. And sometimes they even attack.

FRANKLIN *(lightly):* Sounds like some people I know.

SERAPHINA *(sits back down):* You mean that as a joke. But I believe it.

FRANKLIN *(pause):* I'm curious about something. Why do you pretend to be a . . . ?

SERAPHINA *(finishes his sentence):* Hermit? It's the only way I can keep people from coming up here and nosing around. As long as they think I'm a crazy loner woman, they leave me alone. Except for the sheriff. I think he is in love with the notion of knowing a recluse.

FRANKLIN: Is that why he comes to check on you?

SERAPHINA: I guess. I don't mind once in a while, because it keeps me from having to go down to the store.

FRANKLIN: You really hate people that much?

SERAPHINA: I just got tired of the circus.

FRANKLIN: What do you mean?

SERAPHINA: I used to own a large flower shop. It did very well. After a while, I had a whole chain of shops. But . . . the people . . . I don't know . . . they sometimes . . . overwhelmed me.

FRANKLIN: How do you mean?

SERAPHINA: What do I mean? Let's see, for starters too often when ordinary people become customers, they change. Suddenly somebody's gentle uncle or sweet grandma becomes incredibly demanding and thoughtless. Even verbally brutal. I tried so hard to please. And I succeeded. But at a price. Eventually I pleased all human flesh but me. I became the great pretender. Fear of rejection became a real threat to my happiness and then to my very existence. Somewhere in all the madness I decided it was like a circus act and I just couldn't perform anymore. It was like something I read once:

> *Her eyes died one day*
> *Along with every dream . . .*
> *Another light flowed out*
> *Into an endless, darkened stream.*

And so that is the way it felt. This thing that happened to me.

FRANKLIN: What about family and friends? Weren't they there to help you through this?

SERAPHINA: Well, after some time, my friends and family just sort of eased away from me. I guess I became more trouble than I was worth to them.

FRANKLIN: Don't you ever miss them?

SERAPHINA: Sure. I may be a hermit, but I'm human. But just when I'm about to call one of them from the store, the past slams me back. *(Pause)* You know when I finally decided to give up my business, they thought I was crazy.

They never understood me . . . my needs . . . the stress. What was worse, they never even wanted to get to know the real me. I guess they should have borne another soul. Someone who was fearless with a limitless supply of tolerance and . . . effervescence.

FRANKLIN *(shyly with sincerity):* I . . . think you are quite . . . effervescent.

SERAPHINA: Thank you. But what I possessed was never enough.

FRANKLIN: But don't your friends and family . . . don't they wonder where you are?

SERAPHINA: They all know where I am. A private detective pretending to be a salesman came up here not long after I settled in. About five years ago. They hired him. So they know where I am. But after all this time, there has come a deep silence among us. It isn't full of anger, just a welcomed distance on all sides.

FRANKLIN: But how did you get from the flower shop to this place?

SERAPHINA: Boy, you sure are an inquisitive man. I'm beginning to think my relatives sent you. Did they?

FRANKLIN: No. Of course not. I'm sorry if I'm asking too many questions. It's just that this is all so unusual. I am so . . .

SERAPHINA: Curious?

FRANKLIN: Well, yes. And somehow I can . . .

SERAPHINA *(kindly):* Relate to what I'm talking about?

FRANKLIN: Yes. In fact, those were going to be my exact words.

SERAPHINA: It was just a hunch.

FRANKLIN: Please tell me how you ended up here?

SERAPHINA: Well, I suppose it doesn't matter if you know . . . even if my relatives *did* send you. It's no mystery. One day when I was at my shop . . . I just snapped. It all started with a shipment of flowers that didn't make it in time for a very large wedding. I went into a hyper-panic. I ran into the back room to scream, but then I realized I couldn't let it out. There were too many customers within hearing range. Everywhere I went it seemed there were people. Even in my own home, I knew my neighbors could hear me. Suddenly, I felt trapped. It was like just being alive was suffocating me. I drove out to the country to escape, but even then there were always farmhouses nearby. I frantically realized there were no good places left to scream.

FRANKLIN: How about hollering into your pillow? It has a great muffling effect.

SERAPHINA *(smiling):* And how would you know? Sorry. You don't have to answer that. *(Pause)* By the way, screaming into your pillow doesn't count. At least it doesn't for me. There's no real freedom in that. But here, I have 500 acres to be myself in. I'm free to be afraid, to scream, to hear myself think again, and to watch life . . . without it watching me back like a vulture.

FRANKLIN: So . . . do you still scream?

SERAPHINA: I used to. It felt great. But now, I no longer have the need to.

FRANKLIN: I think a lot of people would benefit from a good scream. You know, a real blood-curdling one. The kind you hear in the movies when the monster is about to attack someone. But no one ever screams. They just end up with nervous tics or a very short fuse. *(Pause)* But still. In all this aloneness. Don't you get . . . lonely?

SERAPHINA: Not often.

FRANKLIN: Don't you want to marry and have a family of your own someday?

SERAPHINA: You mean set up the perfect life like you were trying to do?

FRANKLIN: Yes, only with someone you really love?

SERAPHINA: I suppose it wouldn't be totally out of the question.

FRANKLIN: But how on earth can you do that? How can that ever be even a slight possibility if you live the rest of your life out here?

SERAPHINA *(rises and moves around porch area as she speaks):* Oh, I don't know. Even a hermit can have prospects. I expect a marriage proposal from the sheriff any week now.

FRANKLIN: Do you love him?

SERAPHINA: No. He's not a bad friend, though.

FRANKLIN: Well, if it's not mutual love . . . it's no prospect.

SERAPHINA *(smiling):* Well, you're the expert on that one.

FRANKLIN *(ignoring her comment):* Will you ever leave this place?

SERAPHINA: Perhaps tomorrow . . . perhaps never.

FRANKLIN: Then you will never have your dream of a family.

SERAPHINA *(sits back down):* Who said it was my dream?

FRANKLIN: You did. Somewhere in all your denials.

SERAPHINA: Well, that seems to be another area you are well-versed in. I mean, a courageous man wouldn't have deliberately taken a bad road and then run out of gas. He would have told her the truth. Perhaps you had planned on begging your fiancé's forgiveness for your mistake today.

Then *on* with the wedding. Do you think you'd finally have the courage to tell her on your 10th wedding anniversary that you just married her for her ability to tidy up your life? I can tell you for a fact that women aren't big on those kinds of surprises.

FRANKLIN *(rises from rocking chair and says with a gradual increase in drama):* You may not have much human contact for communicating, but you certainly haven't forgotten how to use your tongue. And I may have lived in denial. But you . . . you are hiding from everything. You say I need courage, but you live a coward's life up here. You wanted to stop the pretending, but your whole existence is a daily lie. Because you were not meant to be a hermit. You are a loving woman full of vibrant life. You should be ashamed of yourself. Your life is too precious to just throw it away out here on these rats. One of the many tragedies is that you will come to the edge of your grave someday and realize that you never fully lived and you never really left anything of value behind. You weren't there to encourage that elderly person who needed your smile. You didn't snuggle with a baby or see the joy of Christmas in your child's eyes. You won't blow out the candles at your 80th birthday party or share a sunset with someone you really care about. You won't have left behind *you,* and all the other lives you would have touched and changed just by your being there. So *what* if life is jammed full of stress? Maybe you should find a career that brings you joy. And there will always be people who can't or just don't want to understand us. It's a maddening pill that everyone seems forced to swallow sometimes. *(Very sincerely)* I know *I've* had to. But we thrive because living is also tempered with the loving grace of a generous Creator. And beyond that, there is this shower of art and nature . . . of kindness, music, laughter . . . and real love. These gifts have been placed everywhere . . . if we're *willing* to open them. Up here maybe screaming works all alone . . . but the sweet gifts of Providence . . . they need to be shared. *(He sits back down, shocked at himself for such a dramatic speech.)*

SERAPHINA *(removes her old sweater and says without anger):* Are you finished?

FRANKLIN *(looks at her somewhat embarrassed):* Yes. Aren't you supposed to be extremely angry? I'm sorry. I don't usually talk in such a *stark* way. In fact, I didn't even know I was capable of that sort of outburst.

SERAPHINA: Actually it was rather interesting to hear something so passionately presented. You are far from bland. I haven't seen a movie, or a play, or a television program in all these five years. You were most . . . entertaining.

FRANKLIN: That's all I was . . . just entertaining?

SERAPHINA: No. That wasn't all. You make me feel lonely. I haven't really felt that . . . until today.

FRANKLIN: I make you feel lonely?

SERAPHINA: Yes. Because when you go, I won't be quite the same. I know that. Did I shock you by saying that?

FRANKLIN (*sincerely*): Yes. But it was a nice kind of jolt.

SERAPHINA: Oh.

FRANKLIN (*pause*): I know what you mean about wanting to be understood. It's priceless. If you find it . . . you can't just toss it away. It's worth too much. (*Thoughtful pause*) Look. The sky is no longer green.

SERAPHINA: The storm passed over without a sigh.

FRANKLIN: But you knew something was coming.

SERAPHINA: I think it *has* come. (*Smiling at him*)

FRANKLIN (*smiling back at her*): I think I know what is here. But it may take awhile to make my life right again. I seem to have made quite a mess. But I know what has to be said. For Anne's sake as well as mine.

SERAPHINA (*sincerely concerned*): It will be painful. Are you certain that's what you want?

FRANKLIN: I shouldn't have kept the truth from her . . . and from me. It was wrong. It will end up hurting us both more this way. As soon as the sheriff comes, I'll take the gas that you offered and find their house. It shouldn't be too hard to find it now. It'll be the one with the shouting people shaking their fists. And it will take a lot of explaining. And I mean a lot. But in time . . . we will all heal.

SERAPHINA: I am sorry for you . . . that you have to pass through this.

FRANKLIN: You know . . . somehow . . . you gave me the courage to do this.

SERAPHINA (*thoughtfully*): There's one for the books. A coward leads the brave parade.

FRANKLIN (*warmly*): You know . . . I don't believe this all was a coincidence. I stumbled up here on your hill for a reason.

SERAPHINA (*smiling*): I don't think I'm going to wrestle you down to the ground arguing that point. (*Thoughtful pause*) Well, until the sheriff comes . . . would you like another piece of cornbread?

FRANKLIN (*lightly affectionate*): I thought you'd never ask . . . Seraphina.

SERAPHINA (*holds back her cornbread from him with a teasing smile*): And are you sure my relatives didn't send you?

FRANKLIN (*genuinely*): Positive.

SERAPHINA (*glowing as she hands basket of cornbread to him*): Well, in that case . . . won't you call me Sarah?

Curtain

PERFORMANCE
LICENSING AGREEMENT

Lillenas Drama Resources
Performance Licensing
P.O. Box 419527, Kansas City, MO 64141

Name _____

Organization _____

Address _____

City _____ State _____ ZIP _____

Circle the Play: The Celestial Helix
                              or
                     Caution to the Wind
                              or
                     No Place to Scream

Number of performances intended _____

Approximate dates _____

Amount remitted* $ _____

Mail to Lillenas at the address above

Order performance copies of this script from your local bookstore or directly
from the publisher at 1-800-877-0700.

*$15.00 for the first performance; $10.00 for each subsequent performance.

Please feel free to photocopy this page.